COUNTRY

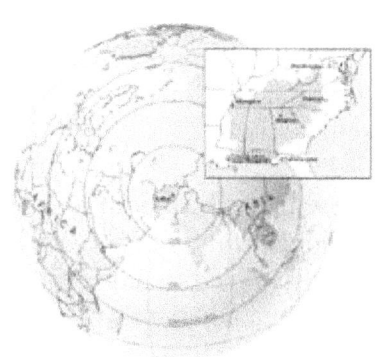

Formal Name: Islamic Republic of Afghanistan (Dowlat-e Eslami-ye-Afghanestan).

Short Form: Afghanistan.

Term for Citizen(s): Afghan(s).

Capital: Kabul.

Major Cities: Herat (Hirat), Jalalabad, Kandahar (Qandahar), Kondoz (Kunduz), and Mazar-e Sharif.

Independence: Afghanistan recognizes its independence day as August 19, the date in 1919 when the country became fully independent of British rule.

Public Holidays: The date of celebration of Afghanistan's Muslim holidays varies because the Islamic calendar is 354 days rather than 365. The holidays in this category are the beginning of Ramadan, Eid al Adha (Feast of the Sacrifice, the end of Ramadan), Ashura (the martyrdom of Imam Hussein), and the birthday of the Prophet Muhammad. Holidays observed on fixed dates include Nawros (New Year's, on the vernal equinox), Victory Day (April 28), and Independence Day (August 19).

Flag: The background of the Afghan flag is three equal vertical sections of black, red, and green from left to right. In the center of the flag in yellow is the national coat of arms, which portrays a mosque with a banner and a sheaf of wheat on either side. In the upper-middle part of the insignia are the lines "There is no God but Allah and Muhammad is his prophet" and "Allah is Great," together with a rising sun. The word "Afghanistan" and the year 1298 (the Muslim calendar equivalent of the year of independence, 1919) are located in the lower part of the insignia.

HISTORICAL BACKGROUND

The Pre-Islamic Period: Archaeological evidence indicates that urban civilization began in the region occupied by modern Afghanistan between 3000 and 2000 B.C. The first historical documents date from the early part of the Iranian Achaemenian Dynasty, which controlled the region from 550 B.C. until 331 B.C. Between 330 and 327 B.C., Alexander the Great defeated the Achaemenian emperor Darius III and subdued local resistance in the territory that is now Afghanistan. Alexander's successors, the Seleucids, continued to infuse the region with Greek cultural influence. Shortly thereafter, the Mauryan Empire of India gained control of southern Afghanistan, bringing with it Buddhism. In the mid-third century B.C., nomadic Kushans established an empire that became a cultural and commercial center. From the end of the Kushan Empire in the third century A.D. until the seventh century, the region was fragmented and under the general protection of the Iranian Sassanian Empire.

The Islamic and Mongol Conquests: After defeating the Sassanians at the Battle of Qadisiya in 637, Arab Muslims began a 100-year process of conquering the Afghan tribes and introducing Islam. By the tenth century, the rule of the Arab Abbasid Dynasty and its successor in Central Asia, the Samanid dynasty, had crumbled. The Ghaznavid Dynasty, an offshoot of the Samanids, then became the first great Islamic dynasty to rule in Afghanistan. In 1220 all of Central Asia fell to the Mongol forces of Genghis Khan. Afghanistan remained fragmented until the 1380s, when Timur consolidated and expanded the existing Mongol Empire. Timur's descendants ruled Afghanistan until the early sixteenth century.

The Pashtun Rulers: In 1504 the region fell under a new empire, the Mughals of northern India, who for the next two centuries contested Afghan territory with the Iranian Safavi Dynasty. With the death of the great Safavi leader Nadir Shah in 1747, indigenous Pashtuns, who became known as the Durrani, began a period of at least nominal rule in Afghanistan that lasted until 1978. The first Durrani ruler, Ahmad Shah, known as the founder of the Afghan nation, united the Pashtun tribes and by 1760 built an empire extending to Delhi and the Arabian Sea. The empire fragmented after Ahmad Shah's death in 1772, but in 1826 Dost Mohammad, the leader of the Pashtun Muhammadzai tribe, restored order.

The Great Game: Dost Mohammad ruled at the beginning of the Great Game, a century-long contest for domination of Central Asia and Afghanistan between Russia, which was expanding to the south, and Britain, which was intent on protecting India. During this period, Afghan rulers were able to maintain virtual independence, although some compromises were necessary. In the First Anglo-Afghan War (1839–42), the British deposed Dost Mohammad, but they abandoned their Afghan garrisons in 1842. In the following decades, Russian forces approached the northern border of Afghanistan. In 1878 the British invaded and held most of Afghanistan in the Second Anglo-Afghan War. In 1880 Abdur Rahman, a Durrani, began a 21-year reign that saw the balancing of British and Russian interests, the consolidation of the Afghan tribes, and the reorganization of civil administration into what is considered the modern Afghan state. During this period, the British secured the Durand Line (1893), dividing Afghanistan from British colonial territory to the southeast and sowing the seeds of future tensions over the division of the Pashtun tribes. Abdur Rahman's son Habibullah (ruled 1901–19) continued his father's administrative reforms and maintained Afghanistan's neutrality in World War I.

Full Independence and Soviet Occupation: In 1919 Afghanistan signed the Treaty of Rawalpindi, which ended the Third Anglo-Afghan War and marks Afghanistan's official date of independence. In the interwar period, Afghanistan again was a balancing point between two world powers; Habibullah's son Amanullah (ruled 1919–29) skillfully manipulated the new British-Soviet rivalry and established relations with major countries. Amanullah introduced his country's first constitution in 1923. However, resistance to his domestic reform program forced his abdication in 1929. In 1933 Amanullah's nephew Mohammad Zahir Shah, the last king of Afghanistan, began a 40-year reign.

After World War II, in which Afghanistan remained neutral, the long-standing division of the Pashtun tribes caused tension with the neighboring state of Pakistan, founded on the other side of the Durand Line in 1948. In response, Afghanistan shifted its foreign policy toward the Soviet Union. The prime ministership of the king's cousin Mohammad Daoud (1953–63) was cautiously reformist, modernizing and centralizing the government while strengthening ties with the Soviet Union. However, in 1963 Zahir Shah dismissed Daoud because his anti-Pakistani policy had damaged Afghanistan's economy.

A new constitution, ratified in 1964, liberalized somewhat the constitutional monarchy. However, in the ensuing decade economic and political conditions worsened. In 1973 Daoud overthrew the king and established a republic. When economic conditions did not improve and Daoud lost most of his political support, communist factions overthrew him in 1978. In 1979 the threat of tribal insurgency against the communist government triggered an invasion by 80,000 Soviet troops, who then endured a very effective decade-long guerrilla war. Between 1979 and 1989, two Soviet-sponsored regimes failed to defeat the loose federation of mujahideen guerrillas that opposed the occupation. In 1988 the Soviet Union agreed to create a neutral Afghan state, and the last Soviet troops left Afghanistan in 1989. The agreement ended a war that killed thousands, devastated industry and agriculture, and created 5 to 6 million refugees.

Civil War and the Taliban: The 1988 agreement did not settle differences between the government and the mujahideen, and in 1992 Afghanistan descended into a civil war that further ravaged the economy. Among the leaders of the warring factions were Ahmad Shah Massoud, an ethnic Tajik; Gulbuddin Hekmatyar, a Pashtun; and Abdul Rashid Dostum, an Uzbek. Despite several temporary alliances, struggles among the armed groups continued until one Islamic fundamentalist group, the Taliban, gained control of most of the country in 1996. The Taliban used an extremist interpretation of Islam to assert repressive control of society. The economy remained in ruins, and most government services ceased.

The Taliban granted the Arab terrorist organization al Qaeda the right to use Afghanistan as a base. As al Qaeda committed a series of international terrorist acts culminating in attacks on the United States on September 11, 2001, the Taliban rejected international pressure to surrender al Qaeda leader Osama bin Laden. When the United States and allies attacked Afghanistan in the fall of 2001, the Taliban government collapsed, but Taliban and al Qaeda leaders escaped. A United States–led International Security Assistance Force began an occupation that is still in place in 2008.

Rebuilding the Country: In December 2001, Afghan leaders in exile signed the Bonn Agreement, forming an interim government, the Afghan Interim Administration, under the leadership of the Pashtun moderate Hamid Karzai. In 2002 Karzai was selected president of the Transitional Islamic State of Afghanistan, whose ruling council included disparate leaders of the anti-Taliban Northern Alliance. A new constitution, written by a specially convened Loya Jirga, or constituent assembly of regional leaders, was ratified in early 2004. In October 2004, an overwhelming popular vote elected Karzai president of the Islamic Republic of Afghanistan. However, regional warlords and large areas of Afghanistan remained beyond the control of the Karzai government. Despite substantial international aid, the Afghan government, which included representatives from many factions, was unable to address numerous social and economic problems. The parliamentary elections of September 2005 gave regional warlords substantial power in both houses of the National Assembly, further jeopardizing Karzai's ability to unite the country. The Bonn Agreement lapsed after the 2005 elections. The agreement's successor, the Afghanistan Compact, went into effect in January 2006 to set goals for international assistance in economic development, security, protection of human rights, and the fight against corruption and drug trafficking through 2010.

In the meantime, the resurgent Taliban intensified terrorist activities in areas beyond government control, particularly the southeastern provinces. In mid-2006, North Atlantic Treaty Organization (NATO) forces turned back a Taliban offensive aimed at Kandahar. However, beginning in 2007 the Taliban utilized safe havens in adjacent Pakistan to gradually restore and expand its control in Afghanistan. In early 2008, it controlled an estimated 10 percent of the country while the government controlled only an estimated 30 percent. Local tribes controlled the remaining territory. Despite U.S.-aided efforts to reduce cultivation of poppies for narcotics production, in 2007 and 2008 that crop accounted for an increasing percentage of Afghanistan's economy and was a major support of the Taliban. In mid-2008, a new International Conference in Support of Afghanistan reaffirmed international commitments to the country's economic and political stability but demanded improved coordination of aid and reduced corruption. Meanwhile, widespread economic hardship increasingly weakened the Karzai government's support among the population.

GEOGRAPHY

Click to Enlarge Image

Location: Afghanistan is located in Central Asia, north and west of Pakistan, east of Iran, and south of Turkmenistan, Uzbekistan, and Tajikistan. The narrow Wakhan Corridor extends from northeasternmost Afghanistan to meet with China.

Size: Afghanistan occupies approximately 647,500 square kilometers, slightly less than Texas.

Land Boundaries: Afghanistan has borders with the following countries: China, 76 kilometers; Iran, 936 kilometers; Pakistan, 2,430 kilometers; Tajikistan, 1,206 kilometers; Turkmenistan, 744 kilometers; and Uzbekistan, 137 kilometers.

Disputed Territory: Afghanistan has no boundary disputes; ongoing incursions, smuggling, and terrorist movement across the Pakistan border are addressed in periodic bilateral meetings.

Length of Coastline/Maritime Claims: Afghanistan is landlocked.

Topography: The terrain of Afghanistan is dominated by rugged mountain ranges, which generally run from the northeast to the southwest. Mountains occupy all but the north-central and southwestern regions of the country, which are dominated by plains. Nearly half the country has an elevation of 2,000 meters or more, and the highest peaks in the northeastern Hindu Kush range exceed 7,000 meters. Historically, mountain passes along the northeastern border with present-day Pakistan have been of great strategic importance. Significant parts of the southwestern plains region are desert.

Principal Rivers: The main rivers are the Amu Darya, 800 kilometers; the Harirud, 850 kilometers; the Helmand, 1,000 kilometers; and the Kabul, 460 kilometers. Afghanistan's chief tributaries to the Amu Darya, which forms much of the country's northern border, are the Koshk and the Qonduz.

Climate: Afghanistan's climate generally is of the arid or semi-arid steppe type, featuring cold winters and dry, hot summers. The mountains of the northeast have subarctic winter conditions. Farther south, monsoon effects moderate the climate near the Pakistan border and increase rainfall as far inland as central Afghanistan. The highest precipitation occurs in the Kabul region of the northeast. The highest temperatures and lowest precipitation are in the southwestern plains region, where summer temperatures reach 49° C. Low temperatures in the northeastern mountains range from –15° C in winter to 0° C in summer. The climate of the north-central Turkistan Plain is increasingly arid closest to the northern borders with Turkmenistan, Uzbekistan, and Tajikistan.

Natural Resources: Agricultural resources are primarily grazing land; fertile crop-growing land is concentrated in Kondoz Province in the north and Helmand Province in the south. Afghanistan is known to have major deposits of chrome, coal, copper, iron, and salt, as well as lesser amounts of a wide variety of minerals including gold, silver, and uranium. Natural gas is the most abundant hydrocarbon resource. Substantial oil deposits are recognized but not yet quantified. Water for all purposes is in critically short supply.

Land Use: Some 12.1 percent of Afghanistan's land is classified as arable; however, in the early 2000s a four-year drought cut that figure in half. In 2007 only 0.2 percent of the total was planted to permanent crops.

Environmental Factors: Although little studied before recent times, the environment of Afghanistan is assumed to have been spared large-scale disturbances until the Soviet invasion of 1979. Since that time, however, numerous events have caused severe damage. Afghanistan, which has no appreciable bodies of water, suffers from a limited freshwater supply that makes potable water unavailable to more than half the population. In recent years, groundwater quality has deteriorated because of agricultural and industrial runoff, and water quantity has been diminished by large-scale land clearing and desertification. Because of insufficient water treatment, the incidence of water-borne diseases is very high. Widespread overgrazing, soil erosion, salinization, and waterlogging have reduced agricultural productivity. Although Afghanistan has little industry, particulate pollutants from the Aral Sea and industrial complexes in Iran, Turkmenistan, and Uzbekistan contaminate the atmosphere in northern Afghanistan. Chemical use and physical destruction in recent military conflicts have damaged the environment, and landmines and unexploded shells are residual hazards endangering an estimated 4 million Afghanis in 32 provinces. Northeastern Afghanistan is considered an earthquake hazard zone; in 1998 an earthquake along the Tajikistan border resulted in an estimated 4,000 fatalities.

Time Zone: Afghanistan is four and one-half hours ahead of Greenwich Mean Time.

SOCIETY

Population: In the early 2000s, population assessment has been difficult because many people have not had fixed residences. In 2008 the estimated population was 32.7 million. The population growth rate was 2.6 percent per year. The population is approximately 75 percent rural; in 2008 the six most populous cities accounted for less than 10 percent of the population. In 2006 net out-migration was 0.4 per 1,000 population. After heavy out-migration and internal displacement in the 1980s and 1990s, an estimated 2.5 million Afghans returned to Afghanistan in 2003–4 before the numbers began to decrease. The United Nations reported that in 2007 some 365,400 Afghanis returned to their country, bringing the total of repatriations since 2002 to 4.1 million. In 2007 more than 2 million Afghans were living in Pakistan and 1.5 million in Iran. In 2007 both countries, the main recipients of Afghan refugees, began preparations for large-scale deportation. Tajikistan closed its border with Afghanistan in 2007. Meanwhile, in that year insecure conditions in Afghanistan noticeably decreased the rate of return. In the early 2000s, hundreds of thousands were internally displaced within Afghanistan, mainly from rural to urban areas, because of drought and instability. In the first quarter of 2008, an estimated 13,000 people fled their homes as conflicts occurred in previously safe regions.

Demography: In 2008 some 44.6 percent of the population was younger than 15 years of age, and 2.4 percent was older than 64. The estimated birthrate was 45.8 per 1,000 population, and the estimated death rate was 19.6 per 1,000 population. The infant mortality rate was 155 deaths per 1,000 live births. Life expectancy was 44.2 years for males and 44.4 years for females. The fertility rate was 6.6 children born per woman.

Ethnic Groups: The main ethnic groups are Pashtun, 42 percent; Tajik, 27 percent; Hazara, 9 percent; Uzbek, 9 percent; Aimak (a Persian-speaking nomadic group), 4 percent; Turkmen, 3 percent; and Baloch, 2 percent. The largest remaining nomadic group is the Kuchis, a Pashtun group whose population has dwindled to about 1.5 million since 1979. The Pashtuns are the major ethnic group in the south and the east, the Tajiks in the northeast. The predominant groups in north-central Afghanistan are the Hazaras, Tajiks, and Uzbeks.

Languages: More than 30 languages are spoken in Afghanistan. The official languages are Dari (Afghan Persian) and Pashtu. Dari is spoken by 50 percent of the population, and Pashtu is spoken as a first language by 35 percent. Turkic languages (primarily Turkmen and Uzbek) are spoken by 11 percent of the population. Of the languages spoken by smaller segments of the population, the most important are Balochi and Pashai. Many Afghans speak more than one language; Dari is the most common second language.

Religion: Virtually the entire population is Muslim. Between 80 and 85 percent of Muslims are Sunni and 15 to 19 percent, Shia. The minority Shia are economically disadvantaged and frequently subjected to discrimination. Small numbers of Hindus and Sikhs live in urban centers. A Jewish population that numbered 5,000 in 1948 had left Afghanistan entirely by 2000.

Education and Literacy: Despite substantial improvements during the reign of Mohammad Zahir Shah (ruled 1933–73), in 1979 some 90 percent of Afghanistan's population was illiterate. In 2006 an estimated 57 percent of men and 87 percent of women were illiterate, and the lack of skilled and educated workers was a major economic disadvantage.

Beginning with the Soviet invasion of 1979, successive wars virtually destroyed the education system. Most teachers fled the country during the Soviet occupation and the subsequent civil war. By 1996 only about 650 schools were functioning. In 1996 the Taliban regime banned education for females, and the madrassa (mosque school) became the main source of primary and secondary education. After the overthrow of the Taliban in 2001, the interim government received substantial international aid to restore the education system, but for the next six years the Taliban attacked public schools wherever possible. In 2007 increased Taliban activity forced the closure of 35 percent of the schools in the southern provinces. The Taliban opened some fundamentalist schools in regions that they controlled. In 2004 and 2005, informal community education programs began in nine provinces. In 2008 about 9,500 schools reportedly were operating, at least some in every province. The Ministry of Education estimated that in 2006, 8 million children were in school, including nearly 3 million girls. Despite renewed emphasis on educating girls, in 2008 the ratio of girls to boys in secondary schools was one to three or four, as rural families continued the tradition of educating only males. Since the end of the dogmatic Taliban era in 2001, public school curricula have included religious subjects, but detailed instruction is left to religious teachers.

Higher education also has been problematic. When Kabul University reopened in 2002, some 24,000 students, male and female, enrolled. In the early 2000s, the rehabilitation of five other universities progressed very slowly. Although seven universities were operating in 2007, only a total of 22,700 students were active in higher education.

Health: Beginning in 1979, military conflict destroyed Afghanistan's health system. Most medical professionals left the country in the 1980s and 1990s, and all medical training programs ceased. In 2003 Afghanistan had 11 physicians and 18 nurses per 100,000 population, and the per capita health expenditure was US$28. In 2004 Afghanistan had one medical facility for every 27,000 people, and some centers were responsible for as many as 300,000 people. In 2007 international organizations provided a large share of medical care. An estimated one-quarter of the population has no access to health care. Neonatal care is especially poor, and infant and child mortality rates are among the highest in the world. In 2005 the number of infant deaths within the first month after birth, 60 per 1,000 live births, was the second-highest rate in the world, and in rural areas, one in five children dies before reaching age five. The maternal death rate, 1,900 per 100,000 live births, also is one of the world's highest.

At the same time, the physical and psychological effects of war have substantially increased the need for medical care. Because of poor sanitation and insufficient potable water supply, infectious and parasitic diseases such as malaria and diarrhea are very common. Malnutrition and poor nutrition also are pervasive. The drought of 1999–2002 exacerbated these conditions. An estimated 800,000 Afghans are disabled. Health authorities consider Afghanistan a high-risk country for human immunodeficiency virus (HIV) because of the high incidence of intravenous drug use, unsafe blood transfusion procedures, large numbers of refugees, poor health facilities, and illiteracy. The comparative impact of those factors is unknown. In 2008 the Ministry of Health reported 435 cases nationwide, but it estimated that a total of 2,000 to 2,500 citizens were currently infected. In 2005 an estimated 1 million people were using narcotics, 200,000 of whom used opium. Despite large-scale international assistance, in 2004 the World Health Organization did not expect Afghanistan's health indicators to improve substantially for at least a decade.

Welfare: Largely because of protracted military conflict, in the early 2000s Afghanistan had the highest proportion of widows and orphans (respectively, 1 million and 1.6 million in 2005) in the world. Large numbers of disabled individuals and former members of regional militias also lack a means of support. The billions of dollars in aid that entered Afghanistan in the post-2001 era tended to bifurcate society as wealth was concentrated in a small elite. In 2006 the British Department for International Development estimated that 70 percent of Afghanis were subsisting on less than US$2 per day. The government has provided very little welfare protection. Most of the welfare activity in the country has been provided by international nongovernmental organizations (NGOs), such as the Afghan Health and Development Services, Afghan Women's Education Center, and Humanitarian Assistance for the Women and Children of Afghanistan, and by United Nations organizations. NGOs also work with Afghan refugees in other countries, especially Pakistan.

ECONOMY

Overview: Economic statistics for Afghanistan traditionally are inexact. Afghanistan's economy, which always has been heavily agricultural and one of the poorest in the world, was shattered by the wars of the 1980s and the 1990s. Industry, much of which depended on agricultural output, suffered as well. After the wars, small-scale trade in urban centers and agriculture in some regions revived quickly. However, damage to the infrastructure will take much longer to repair. In 2007 some 17 provincial reconstruction teams led by Western civilian and military personnel were working to restore economic infrastructure and security in Afghanistan.

Economic recovery achieved since 2001 has been based on large-scale international aid, recovery of the agriculture sector, and substantial growth in the services sector. The 2006 London Conference on Afghanistan pledged US$10.4 billion for economic infrastructure reconstruction during the following three years. In 2008 President Hamid Karzai announced a new five-year National Development Strategy, which includes economic and social components, to be supported by US$50 billion of foreign funds (about half of which had been committed earlier). Donor countries at the International Conference in Support of Afghanistan (Paris, June 2008) pledged US$21 billion for this program over five years. The World Trade Organization began membership negotiations with Afghanistan in 2005; discussions and adjustments were ongoing in 2008, but membership was not expected for several years.

Afghanistan faces a number of serious economic challenges. First and foremost is the need to replace the income generated by opium production, which in 2006 yielded an estimated 53 percent of the country's gross domestic product. Smuggling, particularly across the Pakistan border, also is an important part of the "black economy," which drains resources from the formal economy. Regional disparity of wealth has been severe. Since 2001 Herat, in the conflict-free northwest, has shown economic growth disproportionate to all other cities. By contrast, economic stagnation in most of the country in 2006 and 2007 posed a threat of social unrest that could jeopardize the Karzai government. Privatization, designed to promote economic growth and productivity, was to have been completed in 2009 according to the 2006 Afghanistan Compact, but further efforts in that direction have been officially postponed by the lower house of parliament.

Gross Domestic Product (GDP): Excluding illegal poppy production, for the fiscal year running from March 21, 2006–March 20, 2007, Afghanistan's GDP was estimated at US$8.8 billion or US$270 per capita. In 2006 agriculture contributed an estimated 38 percent to the GDP, services 38 percent, and industry and mining 24 percent. Following the economic standstill of the late 1990s, GDP growth rates in the early 2000s have been very high, although they moderated after reaching 16 percent in 2004 and 14.5 percent in 2005. The growth rate for 2007 was between 7 and 8 percent. However, the starting points upon which such figures are based were very low.

Government Budget: In the early 2000s, Afghanistan's ratio of revenue to gross domestic product was one of the lowest in the world, and domestic revenues were not expected to match the government's operating costs until at least 2011. For the fiscal year running March 21, 2006–March 20, 2007, the proposed operational budget was US$2.6 billion, with predicted revenue of US$715 million plus allotments totaling US$336 million from international trust funds. Thus the budget deficit for that year was about US$1.55 billion. In 2007 increased domestic revenue was considered vital because of anticipated reductions in international aid. The best hope for such improvement was rapid development of mineral resources discovered since 2001.

Inflation: Under the pro-Soviet regimes of the 1980s, inflation was high but limited by government controls. Inflation reached 150 percent per year during the civil war of the early 1990s and is believed to have remained high under the Taliban. After the currency reform of 2002, inflation averaged about 10 percent per year for the first two years, but it rose to 13 percent in 2007.

Agriculture: Agriculture traditionally has been the foundation of Afghanistan's economy, employing as much as 80 percent of the workforce and contributing at least half of the gross domestic product (GDP). Because of the poor quality of most agricultural land, subsistence agriculture predominates. Although many displaced Afghan farmers returned to their land in the early 2000s, land mines and the destruction of irrigation systems had made much agricultural land unusable. Livestock raising, a vital part of the agricultural economy, was similarly affected as grazing land disappeared. The drought of 1999–2002 devastated the rural population and further reduced all types of agricultural output. The nomadic Kuchis were forced to find sedentary occupations. Because of limited water supplies, in the early 2000s half of Afghanistan's arable land was uncultivated. Beginning in 2003, agricultural output increased because of international aid and increased rainfall, except in the south where the drought continued into 2004. The area under cultivation rose significantly in 2004: the area decreased by 21 percent in 2005, but productivity increased. With increased rainfall, 2006 output again increased, but delays in the restoration of irrigation systems hampered the reclaiming of additional agricultural land. The main legal crops are wheat, vegetables, grapes, rice, barley, corn, fruits, and potatoes. The main types of livestock are cattle, sheep, and goats; cow's milk is the most valuable product of livestock raising. In the winter of 2007–8, Afghanistan faced a severe grain shortage, partly because poppy cultivation replaced wheat in some areas, partly because of intensified violence, and partly because of reduced grain imports.

The internationally supported program to replace poppies with legal crops showed progress, mainly in the poorer agricultural regions of the north and west, but in 2006 and 2007 the area and volume of poppy cultivation increased substantially in the richer soils of the south, especially in Helmand Province. Wheat was the main replacement crop. Overall, the volume of poppy output increased by 59 percent in 2006 and by 34 percent in 2007. The program to end poppy cultivation suffered from poor regional cooperation, opium growers often were not compensated for lost crops, and in key areas poppies continued to be more economically viable than alternative crops.

Forestry: Most of Afghanistan's mountains are barren rather than forested. In the mid-1990s, an estimated 2.9 percent of the land was forested, but since that time war, illegal exploitation, and the need for firewood have removed as much as 90 percent of that resource. There is no program of forest preservation or commercial exploitation. In 2005 an estimated 3.2 million cubic meters of timber was harvested, about 45 percent of which was used for fuel.

Fishing: Afghanistan has no appreciable fishing industry. In 2005 the catch totaled about 900 tons of fish.

Mining and Minerals: Most of Afghanistan's mineral resources, which are believed to be substantial, remain unexploited. In 2008 a U.S. Geological Survey study began identifying new resource locations. Among resources previously identified are bauxite, emeralds, gold, iron, lead, magnesium, mercury, silver, sulfur, tin, uranium, and zinc. Because of transportation problems, regional conflict, inaccessible terrain, and insufficient investment, only barites, chromium, coal, copper, natural gas, and salt have been extracted commercially. Before the Soviet invasion, natural gas was the most important natural resource export. In 2008 the China Metallurgical Group's lease of the Aynak Valley, which contains extensive copper deposits, opened the potential for Afghanistan's mineral wealth to significantly improve the national economy. A large iron deposit discovered in 2008 at Hajigag in Bamiyan Province is scheduled to be leased to a private company for extraction to begin in 2009. A substantial new coal reserve also was discovered in 2008 in Bamiyan Province. The largest coal mining operation is at Karkar Dodkash in north-central Afghanistan.

Industry and Manufacturing: Before the wars of the late twentieth century, industry was based on the processing of local agricultural products, including textiles, sugar, and chemical fertilizers made from natural gas or coal. The main manufacturing center was the Kabul region. In 2004 all of Afghanistan's industrial sector had stopped producing or was producing at a substantially reduced rate. The reasons for this reduction in productivity are war damage, shortages of raw materials and spare parts, and the postwar priority of rebuilding overall infrastructure before industry. In the early 2000s, foreign investment in the industrial sector focused on small and medium-sized enterprises, predominantly in telecommunications. Revival projects have concentrated on agricultural processing and carpet enterprises. In 2007 the carpet industry, which provides the most valuable legal export commodity, employed an estimated 1 million people directly. The supply of raw materials for that industry employed at least the same number. Some small plants in Herat, Kabul, and Mazar-e Sharif produce textiles, leather goods, and processed foods. Because of war damage, the construction sector expanded rapidly in the early 2000s and was seen as an important economic driver for the ensuing decade. However, that sector of the economy suffers from substantial corruption.

Energy: War damage depleted Afghanistan's energy generation infrastructure, particularly generators and power lines. Some natural gas wells and 31 oil wells that were active during the Soviet occupation have remained capped since that era. In 2004 energy shortages were a critical obstacle in resuming economic activity, but between 2005 and 2008 the electricity supply improved under Minister of Water and Energy Ismail Khan. Reconstruction of the Kajaki Dam on the Helmand River in south-central Afghanistan, begun in 2005, aims to provide electricity to an additional 3 million people and to expand the existing irrigation system in the region. Turkmenistan, Tajikistan, and Uzbekistan have sent electric power to some northern regions of Afghanistan. In August 2008, Afghanistan signed an agreement for construction of new lines bringing electric power from Kyrgyzstan and Tajikistan to Afghanistan and Pakistan by 2013, within a new regional energy grouping, the Central Asia/South Asia Regional Electricity Market. In 2008 Turkmenistan also signed a new agreement to supply natural gas.

Given adequate extraction and distribution infrastructure, Afghanistan's domestic coal, natural gas, and oil resources can meet its energy needs, and the Kunar River provides untapped hydroelectric potential. In 2004 natural gas reserves were estimated at 5 trillion cubic feet. In the early 2000s, oil reserves were estimated at 95 million barrels and coal reserves at 73 million tons, but substantially larger oil reserves have been identified in the Amu Darya Basin and the Afghan-Tajik Basin north of Kabul. Resumed extraction of natural gas, once a key export, is a top economic priority. Afghanistan is a natural pipeline route between Central Asian natural gas fields and the Arabian Sea, and the often-discussed Trans-Afghan Pipeline clearly would be an economic boon to Afghanistan, but the line would pass through territory controlled in 2007 and 2008 by the Taliban. Hence, security issues have prevented construction since the original agreement was signed in 2002 by Afghanistan, Pakistan (the chief consumer), and Turkmenistan (the supplier). Afghanistan's domestic pipelines connect gas fields only with local consumers and the Mazar-e-Sharif power plant.

Services: Afghanistan's banking system, which collapsed during the civil war of the early 1990s, was limited to financial transactions supporting retail commerce. With the collapse, money-changers became the main source of financing, and opium and wheat became the primary forms of capital for the agricultural population. Elimination of poppy cultivation would mean destitution for many farmers relying on opium for credit. Since 2002 the government has encouraged recovery of a formal banking system. New commercial banking laws were passed in 2003, and banks from Britain, India, and Pakistan opened branches in Kabul. In mid-2004 the

Afghanistan International Bank (AIB) began operating with the backing of the Asian Development Bank and 75 percent ownership by Afghan businessmen.

The smuggling and other illegal economic activity that were pervasive during the war periods left a very strong residual black-market economy specializing in exporting goods illegally into Pakistan and moving illegal drugs northward into Central Asia and ultimately Russia and Western Europe. The opium production supporting the latter activity remained very high (accounting for an estimated 93 percent of the world supply in 2007), despite government efforts to reduce it.

Because security conditions in Afghanistan have remained inadequate, especially outside Kabul, the formerly prosperous tourism industry had not revived as of 2008, despite a government program to establish 20 tourist sites by 2010. Meanwhile, dangerous conditions have spurred the growth of private security services that protect government officials and businesspeople.

Labor: Because of the very large black-market economy, statistics on the labor force are incomplete. In 2004 the labor force in the legitimate economy was estimated at 15 million, of whom about 28 percent were women. The conflicts of the 1980s and 1990s seriously depleted the supply of skilled labor. According to a 2004 estimate, about 80 percent of the workforce was in agriculture, 10 percent in industry, and 10 percent in services. Although accurate statistics on unemployment generally have not been available, two 2005 estimates were 40 and 50 percent, respectively. No minimum wage has been set. Existing labor laws are little observed, and unions have not played a role in protecting workers' rights.

Foreign Economic Relations: The United States has given Afghanistan status as a least-developed beneficiary developing nation, which removes tariffs on several U.S. imports from Afghanistan. In 2004 the United States signed a bilateral Trade and Investment Framework Agreement, which increased trade levels with Afghanistan. In 2007 a joint statement under that agreement created a new framework for bilateral commercial cooperation. The European Union also gives Afghan products preferential trade status. Trade with Iran has increased substantially in the post-Taliban era. Iran has given Afghanistan the use of its Arabian Sea port at Chabahar under favorable conditions, despite U.S. objections. In 2003 Afghanistan, Iran, and Uzbekistan established a trans-Afghan trade corridor linking Uzbekistan with Chabahar and Bandar-e Abbas. Uzbekistan's border procedures have slowed commerce along the route, however. Trade with Pakistan is complicated by a high level of smuggling across the border; in 2004 an estimated 80 percent of goods entering Afghanistan from Pakistan were subsequently smuggled back into Pakistan. The volume of that commerce was estimated in 2007 at US$10 billion, compared with US$2 billion of legitimate trade between the two countries. In 2002 the two countries revived their Joint Economic Commission, which had been moribund for 10 years, in order to improve commercial relations. The commission has not met regularly in the ensuing years, however.

In 2006 the main purchasers of Afghanistan's exports in order of volume were India, Pakistan, the United States, and Britain. The main suppliers of Afghanistan's imports in order of volume were Pakistan, the United States, Germany, and India. The main legal export commodities were fruits and nuts, carpets, wool, cotton, hides and pelts, and precious and semi-precious gems. The main imports were capital goods, food, textiles, and petroleum products. Afghanistan's foreign trade increased substantially in volume in the early 2000s. In the fiscal year ending in March 2007, Afghanistan's exports (not including re-exports) were worth US$274 million, and imports were valued at US$3.8 billion, creating an unfavorable trade balance of about US$3.5 billion.

Balance of Payments: For fiscal year 2004, Afghanistan had a balance of payments surplus of US$131 million, mainly because of US$2.7 billion in international grants. More recent financial statistics were not available as of 2008. In 2006 Afghanistan had US$1.9 billion in foreign-currency reserves.

External Debt: In 2006 Afghanistan had US$11.9 billion in external debt, but in 2007 it qualified for World Bank assistance under the Heavily Indebted Poor Countries Initiative. That program cut the net public and private debt by 51 percent.

Foreign Investment: To encourage foreign investment, in 2002 the government began allowing 100 percent foreign ownership of Afghan enterprises, offering substantial tax benefits and unlimited transfer of assets out of the country. The Afghanistan Investment Support Agency was established in 2003 to centralize foreign investment activities. However, Afghanistan's highly corrupt and inefficient bureaucracy has limited investment, there is no legal system for adjudication of commercial disputes, there is significant resentment in the provinces against foreign intrusion, and the government has passed no significant reforms. In addition, the liberalized ownership policy does not apply to investment in pipeline construction, telecommunications infrastructure, the fuels and minerals industries, or other heavy industry where state-owned enterprises predominate. In 2006 the World Bank's international rating on business conditions rated Afghanistan number 162 in the world, in part because of security conditions. The city of Herat, located in the conflict-free northwest, has attracted an estimated US$350 million in investment since 2001, far more than any other city. Likely future investment sectors are telecommunications, energy, mining, agricultural equipment, and health care systems. In 2006 Coca-Cola opened a US$25 million bottling plant in Kabul. In 2007 two Chinese companies agreed to invest US$3.7 billion for access to the Aynak Valley copper deposits, the largest single foreign investment ever made in Afghanistan. Other large investors include Pakistan, Iran, the United Arab Emirates, Central Asian countries, members of the European Union, and the United States.

Currency and Exchange Rate: In late August 2008, the exchange rate of the afghani was 50.1 to the U.S. dollar. The rate has remained relatively stable since the currency reform of 2002. Acceptance of the afghani has been gradual, and in 2008 many foreign currencies were in circulation.

Fiscal Year: The fiscal year begins March 21.

TRANSPORTATION AND TELECOMMUNICATIONS

Overview: Afghanistan's transportation system, which prior to 1979 was rudimentary except for a modern system of main roads, suffered severe damage during the ensuing two decades. In the post-2001 era, the weak transportation infrastructure has been a major deterrent to realizing

Afghanistan's potential as a regional commercial crossroads. The road system, which provides the only transport in most parts of the country, has been an urgent reconstruction project. Some 79 percent of public transport expenditures for the period 2005–11 are earmarked for road improvement. No rail system exists. After suffering damage to most airports during the wars, the air transport system has been reviving in the early 2000s. Because landlocked Afghanistan has been very dependent on routes through Pakistan, with which relations have been tense, a top priority is diversifying Afghanistan's access to seaports and to new markets in India by making new bilateral transportation agreements.

Roads: The main internal road system that was built in the 1960s included about 2,000 kilometers of roads. After an intensive international road-building and restoration effort, in 2008 Afghanistan had an estimated 13,100 kilometers of paved roads. However, even in Kabul the condition of many roads still was poor in 2008 as reconstruction lagged. Heavily damaged in the 1980s and 1990s, the main arteries connect the cities of Ghazni, Herat, Kabul, and Kandahar with roads crossing the Pakistan border. Critical commercial and military roadways through the Salang and Tang-e Gharu mountain passes, north and east of Kabul, respectively, were badly damaged during the Soviet occupation and ensuing conflicts. As of 2008, some parts of the so-called Ring Road network, which would link most population and commercial centers, had been completed. That includes a highway connecting Kabul with Kandahar, but a connector between Kandahar and Herat, begun in 2004, was not yet complete in 2008. Germany is financing a road connecting Jalalabad with the Pakistan border. India, Iran, and Pakistan are constructing roads connecting Afghanistan with their respective national road systems. One such route is to connect Iran's port of Chabahar on the Gulf of Oman with Tajikistan via Afghanistan. Provincial roads, which also received heavy damage during conflicts of recent decades, generally have not been repaired since the end of hostilities.

Railroads: In 2008 Afghanistan had no functioning railroads. For a variety of geopolitical and practical reasons, numerous plans for a trans-Afghan line failed to materialize in the nineteenth and twentieth centuries. Only five short domestic lines were built, including one line passing across the Friendship Bridge into Uzbekistan. Otherwise, lines built toward Afghanistan by surrounding countries stopped at the border. In the early 2000s, road building was a much higher priority of infrastructure restoration than railroad building. Only US$100,000 of public transport funding for the period 2005–11 was earmarked for railroad construction. In 2006 plans called for five new freight dispatch stations along the borders to link domestic roads with rail lines from neighboring countries. In 2008 construction was underway on a 189-kilometer rail line linking Herat with the east Iranian town of Sangan.

Ports: Afghanistan is landlocked; the main ports along its chief waterway, the Amu Darya River, are Kheyrabad and Shir Khan.

Inland Waterways: The most important inland waterway is the Amu Darya River, whose 800 kilometers along Afghanistan's border can accommodate vessels up to 500 deadweight tons.

Civil Aviation and Airports: In 2007 some 46 airports were in operation; 12 had paved runways, but only four had runways longer than 3,000 meters. Nine heliports also were in operation. In 2006 Kabul International Airport, the only destination for international flights into

Afghanistan, began a major reconstruction project with Japanese aid. Its new international terminal was to be operational in late 2008. Also in late 2008, the North Atlantic Treaty Organization (NATO)–led International Security Assistance Force was scheduled to begin turning over air traffic control at Kabul International to civilian operators. Connections to Kabul are made via Delhi, India; Islamabad, Pakistan; and Baku, Azerbaijan. Airports at Herat, Jalalabad, and Mazar-e Sharif also were renovated in the early 2000s. The military conflicts of 1979–2001 destroyed many of the aircraft of the national line, Ariana, and damaged most of the civilian airports. In 2004 Ariana began regular flights to Delhi, Dubai, Frankfurt, Islamabad, Istanbul, and Moscow. In 2003 Afghanistan's first private airline, Kam Air, began flights. However, in 2005 both Ariana and Kam were banned in airports of the European Union because of poor safety standards. In 2008 Ariana's fleet included eight airliners; delivery of four more was scheduled for 2009. Beginning in 2002, Afghanistan's civilian aviation has received substantial foreign assistance; India has trained flight staff and contributed three Airbuses.

Pipelines: In 2007 Afghanistan had 466 kilometers of natural gas pipelines.

Telecommunications: In 2004 Afghanistan had an estimated 50,000 main telephone lines and 600,000 cellular phones. Mobile phones, introduced to Afghanistan in 2001, became the principal means of communication in the early 2000s, as expansion of landline services virtually stopped. In 2006 an estimated 3.2 million mobile phone subscriptions were active. By 2008, four mobile phone companies were in operation. Plans call for establishment of a unified countrywide mobile phone network based on code division multiple access technology, in cooperation with U.S. and Chinese companies. The number of Afghans with Internet access increased rapidly between 2000 and 2008, multiplying from an estimated 1,000 to 580,000. Public Internet facilities are available in Herat, Kabul, Kandahar, and Mazar-e Sharif. In many areas, however, unpredictable power cuts hinder Internet access.

GOVERNMENT AND POLITICS

Overview: The adoption of a new constitution in January 2004 and the election of Hamid Karzai as president in October 2004 were considered major advances in Afghanistan's fragmented political life. However, day-to-day control of the provinces proved difficult both before and after the election, and substantial regional power centers remained in 2008. After the first National Assembly was seated in December 2005, the balance between the executive and legislative branches was uncertain, and Karzai has been obliged to award cabinet positions to key regional warlords. The role of Islamic precepts in governance remains extremely controversial, particularly in the judicial branch. In March 2008, the United Nations continued its policy of one-year renewals of its Assistance Mission in Afghanistan, designed to coordinate international aid and guide the rebuilding process.

Executive Branch: The president and two vice presidents are elected as a ticket by popular vote to five-year terms. The first such election under the 2004 constitution occurred in October 2004. President Hamid Karzai, who was elected at that time, is both chief of state and head of government. The president appoints ministers, subject to the approval of the Wolesi Jirga (People's Council), the lower house of the National Assembly. Following a reorganization in early 2006, the government included 25 ministries; appointments to these ministries have been distributed among influential regional and military groups. The reorganization of 2006 reduced the number of ministries by two and shifted key individuals. One woman headed a ministry in 2008. The national security adviser and the governor of the central bank have ministerial status in the government. The National Defense Commission, headed by Karzai, is a six-member advisory board that includes leaders of the main regional groups. Karzai has attempted to manipulate key regional individuals and groups to maintain a base of power. An example is Karzai's careful treatment of Abdul Rashid Dostum, a powerful Uzbek warlord considered vital in holding northern Afghanistan against the Taliban. That strategy has involved Karzai in complex regional power struggles. He has been accused of supporting certain opium traffickers in exchange for support in southern provinces.

Legislative Branch: The constitution calls for a bicameral legislature, the National Assembly. Members of the lower house, the 249-member Wolesi Jirga (People's Council), are elected directly for five-year terms. The next election is scheduled for 2010. The Wolesi Jirga has 249 seats, whose geographical allocation is determined by population. Some 68 seats are designated for women and 10 for the Kuchis, a large seminomadic group. The 102 members of the upper house, the Meshrano Jirga (House of Elders), are appointed by provincial councils (one member for each of 34 provinces, serving four-year terms); by district councils (accounting for another 34 members, each serving three-year terms); and the president (34 members who serve five-year terms). The constitution specifies that the presidential appointees be one-half women and include two representatives of the Kuchis and two representatives of the disabled. Members of the Meshrano Jirga are appointed after the elections for the Wolesi Jirga. The government can convene a Loya Jirga (Constituent Assembly) to decide urgent matters of independence, national sovereignty, and territorial integrity. Such an assembly, which can amend the constitution and bring charges against the president, must include members of the National Assembly and chairpersons of the provincial and district councils. A 1,650-member Loya Jirga chose the transitional government that took office in 2002, and a second such council formulated the 2004 constitution.

Judicial Branch: Afghanistan's judicial branch deteriorated during the Soviet occupation, and justice was administered by strict Islamic law during the Taliban era (1996–2001). To replace the ad hoc system in place under the transitional government, the constitution of 2004 stipulated that the Supreme Court include nine justices appointed by the president, with approval of the Wolesa Jirga, for 10-year terms. Those justices have particular importance because they are responsible for managing the personnel, budgets, and policy decisions of the entire national, regional, and local court system. At the urging of his Western partners in the 2006 Afghanistan Compact, President Karzai replaced several Supreme Court justices in 2006. Also in 2006, the Wolesa Jirga refused the renomination of the ultraconservative Fazel Hadi Shinwari, a staunch advocate of Islamic law, as chief justice. However, his replacement, Abdul Salam Azimi, proved equally conservative in his first two years on the court. At the level below the Supreme Court are high and appeals courts. A National Security Court handles cases of terrorism and other threats to national security.

Administrative Divisions: The major subnational administrative division is the province (*wilayat*), numbering 34 in 2008. The two newest provinces were added in 2004. Each province has between five and 15 districts. In 2006 some 361 districts were in existence, but the number changes frequently as districts split or combine. Each province has one designated provincial municipality; some but not all provinces also have a single rural municipality. The municipalities fall under the direct jurisdiction of the Ministry of Interior.

Provincial and Local Government: According to the constitution, provinces, districts, and villages are governed by directly elected councils. The first elections for those councils, which totaled 420 seats, were held concurrently with the national parliamentary elections of September 2005. The chief executive at the province level is the governor, who is appointed by the president. As is the case with the national cabinet, the president has distributed governorships among influential regional and military groups. Province and district administrations have the same basic structure as the national government. According to the constitution of 2004, the central government, which theoretically stands at the center of a highly centralized system, delegates authority to the subnational jurisdictions in (unspecified) matters where local or regional action is more efficient. In actuality, the structure and government of the provinces have varied greatly; in most cases, provincial governance is based on the financial and military strength of local leaders as well as personal and tribal loyalties. In some southern jurisdictions, the Taliban insurgency has been able to establish parallel governments, including administrators and judges.

Judicial and Legal System: Although every province has a lower and a higher court, judicial procedures are influenced by local authorities and traditions. The supply of trained jurists is very limited. In 2002 the transitional government established an education program run by Italian judicial experts to prepare judges, prosecutors, and defense lawyers. Although some individuals received secular judicial training in the early 2000s, the majority of local court officials came from Muslim religious schools and lacked judicial skills. The respective roles of Islamic and secular law in the new national judicial system have not been well established; a large portion of the current law code is based on laws passed under the last king, Mohammad Zahir Shah (ruled 1933–73). In rural areas, where local elders and tribal authorities resolve criminal cases, Taliban laws have remained in effect. According to a 2006 estimate, in all provinces some 90 percent of local cases are based on Islamic and tribal law.

Electoral System: Suffrage is universal for male and female citizens 18 years of age and older. A new electoral and political party law went into effect in May 2004. About 77 percent of registered voters participated in the direct presidential election of 2004, the first since 1969. That election was managed by the Interim Election Commission appointed by Hamid Karzai, then the head of the interim government. Although some incidents of intimidation were reported in elections for the constitutional Loya Jirga in late 2003, the constitutional referendum of January 2004, and the presidential election of October 2004, monitors found those voting processes to be basically fair. In 2004 Karzai appointed an 11-member Joint Electoral Management Body to permanently oversee election registration and procedures. The first parliamentary and local elections were held in September 2005 after being postponed for nearly a year for security reasons. Although the election commission ostensibly disqualified individuals commanding armed groups from the parliamentary elections, several of the most powerful regional warlords gained seats. The complex voting system for those elections, in which about 50 percent of eligible voters participated, received substantial criticism. Because all candidates ran as individuals and no party representation was allowed, substantial fragmentation of parliamentary coalitions resulted. The next presidential election is scheduled for 2009 and the next parliamentary election for 2010.

Politics and Political Parties: The Political Parties Law of 2003 requires that all political parties be registered with the Ministry of Justice and observe the precepts of Islam. In 2007 some 82 parties had gained such recognition. Because party identification was not allowed for candidates in the 2005 elections, party-based coalitions could not function in parliament. Most political groupings are based on alliances that formed during the military struggles of 1979–2002. The Northern Alliance is an influential loose confederation of several Hazara, Tajik, and Uzbek groups who fought against the Taliban. Factions of the alliance were key forces in the parliament elected in 2005. In 2008 the largest individual parties were the Islamic Party of Afghanistan, the National Congress Party of Afghanistan (represented in the presidential election by fifth-place finisher Abdul Latif Pedram), the National Islamic Movement of Afghanistan (an Uzbek party, represented in the election by fourth-place finisher Abdul Rashid Dostum), the National Movement of Afghanistan (a coalition of 11 parties also known as the Afghan Nationalist Party), the Islamic Society of Afghanistan, the Islamic Unity Party, and the United National Front (founded by members of the Northern Coalition and other leaders after the 2005 elections). United National Front member Yonous Qanooni, the speaker of the Wolesi Jirga, has been a key voice of opposition to the Karzai government and is considered a likely candidate in the 2009 presidential election. President Karzai has declined to form a party to advance his programs. The first parliament featured a broad division between leaders of previous military conflicts and younger "modernists" who emphasized future development of the country. Another important division of political power is between the Pashtun-dominated south and the Tajik- and Uzbek-dominated north.

Mass Media: In 2005 Afghanistan had an estimated 45 FM radio stations and about 10 television stations. Radio is the most widespread source of information. In 2003 an estimated 37 percent of Afghan citizens, mainly in urban centers, had access to a local radio station. A government-run national television station and seven radio stations were located in Kabul, and nine provinces had regional television stations. Most of the electronic news media are government-owned. In the early 2000s, state-owned Radio Television Afghanistan was the most powerful broadcast outlet. Four cable stations appeared after the overthrow of the Taliban, carrying Indian and U.S. programs. By 2005, the private station Tolo TV had achieved great popularity by airing Western-style programs that occasionally ran afoul of Islamic critics. The private radio station Radio Arman followed a similar trajectory. As their public access increased, the broadcast media received increasing pressure from conservative Islamic factions. Prominent media figures were murdered in 2005 and 2007. Some government officials have used their positions to maintain their own communications facilities.

The circulation of independent print publications has been confined to the Kabul region. The 2004 media law requires registration of periodicals with the Ministry of Information and Culture; in 2005 some 250 periodicals were registered. The principal daily newspapers are the state-owned *Anis*, *Eslah*, and *Kabul Times* and the privately owned *Arman-e Melli*, *Eradeh*, *Hewad*, *Ittefaq-e Islam*, and *Shari'at*. Because of financial difficulties, all independent print media are dependent on the government or a political faction. Domestic news agencies are the state-owned Bakhtar and the privately owned Hindokosh and Kabul Press.

Foreign Relations: Traditionally a neutral country, Afghanistan mirrored the foreign policy of the Soviet Union during the decade of Soviet occupation (1979–89). Neither the Soviet-supported regimes in Afghanistan nor the Taliban regime (respectively, 1979–89 and 1996–2001) received wide international recognition. After the fall of the Taliban in 2001, Afghanistan established diplomatic relations with most countries of the world. In December 2002, the six nations bordering Afghanistan signed a "Good Neighbor Declaration," guaranteeing the country's independence and territorial integrity.

Since its establishment in 1948 on Afghanistan's southeastern border, Pakistan has been a key neighbor with which Afghanistan has had substantial differences. During the Soviet occupation, Pakistan was the main supply point for the mujahideen insurgency. In the late 1990s, Pakistan supported the Taliban regime, reversing its support only after the Taliban refused to surrender Osama bin Laden in late 2001. Long-term relations between Afghanistan and Pakistan have been strained by the ongoing separation of the Pashtun tribes and by disagreements on border procedures and smuggling. A United States–sponsored Tripartite Commission is the main arena for discussion of these issues. Major ongoing issues are the continued presence of Taliban and al Qaeda forces in Pakistan's border provinces and Afghanistan's willingness to have closer relations with India. In 2008 relations were strained further when President Hamid Karzai implicated Pakistan in an assassination attempt on him and threatened to pursue Taliban forces into Pakistan. In an effort to improve border security, in early 2008 the first of six small U.S.-Afghan-Pakistani border security posts was opened on the Afghanistan–Pakistan border. Both partners have a vital stake in friendly relations: for Afghanistan, Pakistan remains a vital corridor to the Arabian Sea, and for Pakistan, Afghanistan is a vital connection to the hydrocarbon and other resources of Central Asia. In the early 2000s, Pakistan's archenemy India has moved aggressively by offering Afghanistan a range of assistance projects and establishing diplomatic missions throughout Afghanistan.

Relations with Iran generally have been positive. Iran opposed the Soviet-backed and Taliban regimes in Afghanistan, and it has actively supported reconstruction efforts of the early 2000s. Trade relations also have improved in this period. The main bilateral issue is Iran's long-standing claim to share the water resources of the Helmand River, which irrigates Afghanistan's southern agricultural region before flowing into Iran. Other issues are the ongoing presence of Afghan refugees in Iran and Iranian concerns for the Shia minority in Afghanistan. Beginning in 2005, the Karzai government felt substantial Western pressure to eschew closer relations with Iran, which in turn endeavored to create new bilateral links. Suspected Iranian shipments of military matériel to insurgent groups in Afghanistan became an issue in 2007.

Russia has viewed Afghanistan as a vital region since the early nineteenth century. Relations with the Soviet Union were close until the invasion of 1979, which aroused lasting hostility on the Afghan side. In the early 2000s, official relations have improved as Russia pledged assistance in building Afghanistan's military and business establishments, clearing landmines, and developing oil and gas extraction. However, residual mistrust and issues such as outstanding

Soviet-era debts to Russia, which Afghanistan has not officially recognized, have limited improvement.

Relations with post-Soviet Tajikistan were complicated by Afghanistan's role in its neighbor's long civil war of the 1990s. Tajik insurgents used Afghanistan as a base for military operations, and about 100,000 Tajiks took refuge in northern Afghanistan in the early 1990s. In the early 2000s, Afghanistan sought improved commercial relations; the Tajik-Afghan Friendship Bridge was completed over the Amu Darya River in 2004 to enhance the trade route north into Tajikistan. Relations with Uzbekistan have been limited by the harsh border controls enforced by Uzbekistan to prevent the entry of narcotics smugglers and Islamic fundamentalists from the south and by Uzbekistan's ongoing support for Abdul Rashid Dostum, the Uzbek warlord who controls parts of northeastern Afghanistan. In 2008 Afghanistan joined Kyrgyzstan, Pakistan, and Tajikistan in a new Inter-Governmental Council to oversee the transmission of electric power within the new Central Asia/South Asia Regional Electricity Market.

Afghanistan grew in importance for the United States because of the Soviet invasion of 1979, but the Soviet occupation, ensuing civil war, and Taliban regime made normal relations difficult or impossible until the fall of the Taliban in late 2001. Since that time, the successive Karzai governments have received substantial U.S. support to reestablish infrastructure and strengthen government control in outlying regions. The United States has granted Afghanistan considerable preferential trade treatment. Since entering Afghanistan in late 2001, the U.S.-led Operation Enduring Freedom and increasing numbers of U.S. troops in the North Atlantic Treaty Organization (NATO)–led International Security Assistance Force have pursued the objectives of eliminating Taliban and al Qaeda forces from Afghanistan and providing humanitarian assistance.

Membership in International Organizations: Afghanistan belongs to the following international organizations: the Asian Development Bank, Colombo Plan, Economic Cooperation Organization, Food and Agriculture Organization of the United Nations, Group of 77, International Atomic Energy Agency, International Bank for Reconstruction and Development, International Civil Aviation Organization, International Criminal Police Organization (Interpol), International Development Association, International Federation of Red Cross and Red Crescent Societies, International Finance Corporation, International Fund for Agricultural Development, International Labour Organization, International Monetary Fund, International Organization for Migration, International Telecommunication Union, Islamic Development Bank, Multilateral Investment Guarantee Agency, Organisation for the Prohibition of Chemical Weapons, Organization for Security and Co-operation in Europe (cooperative partner), Organization of the Islamic Conference, United Nations, United Nations Committee on Trade and Development, United Nations Educational, Scientific and Cultural Organization, United Nations Industrial Development Organization, Universal Postal Union, World Federation of Trade Unions, World Health Organization, and World Trade Organization (observer status).

Major International Treaties: Afghanistan is a signatory to the following multilateral agreements: Comprehensive Test Ban Treaty; Convention on Biological Diversity; Convention on the International Trade in Endangered Species of Wild Flora and Fauna; Convention on the Prohibition of Military or Any Other Hostile Use of Environmental Modification Techniques;

conventions prohibiting the development, production, stockpiling, and use of biological and chemical weapons (known, respectively, as the Biological Weapons Convention and the Chemical Weapons Convention); Geneva Conventions; Montreal Protocol on Substances That Deplete the Ozone Layer; Treaty on the Non-Proliferation of Nuclear Weapons; United Nations Convention to Combat Desertification; and United Nations Framework Convention on Climate Change. Afghanistan has signed but not ratified the Basel Convention on the Control of Transboundary Movements of Hazardous Wastes and Their Disposal, Convention on Fishing and Conservation of Living Resources of the High Seas, and United Nations Convention on the Law of the Sea. As of April 2008, Afghanistan had not signed the Kyoto Protocol to the United Nations Framework Convention on Climate Change.

NATIONAL SECURITY

Overview: Beginning with the accession of the Karzai government in 2004, national security policy has aimed to establish a credible armed force, the Afghan National Army (ANA), and a national police force that will provide all conventional aspects of domestic security. In 2008 some 35,000 soldiers had been trained by U.S. forces and participated in counterterrorism operations, but the air force, still in the formative stage, had only 1,400 technical and logistical personnel. Afghanistan, a landlocked nation, has no navy. The long-term goal has been to prepare an army of 70,000 (in five corps), an air force of 8,000, a border guard force of 12,000, and a police force of 82,000. However, a 2008 revision calls for increasing the army to 120,000 by 2013. The National Security Directorate, the national intelligence agency, is administered by the Ministry of Interior. In 2006 the government estimated that 10,000 militia organizations existed, many of them commanded by regional warlords. A series of amnesty programs have disarmed some militia units and reintegrated them into society, but the elimination of militias remains an elusive goal of the central government. Much territory remains outside government control and is dominated by narcotics traffickers, tribal leaders, and insurgent groups. In 2007–8 trafficking and insurgent groups in the south continued to increase their cooperation; the Taliban's 2007 income from opium trafficking was estimated at US$100 million.

Foreign Military Relations: Afghanistan has depended almost entirely on U.S. and North Atlantic Treaty Organization (NATO) forces, known, respectively, as Operation Enduring Freedom and the International Security Assistance Force (ISAF), to provide security in and around Kabul and to combat Taliban forces elsewhere in Afghanistan. In 2008 the ISAF, which since 2003 has been under the rotating command of officers from NATO countries, included about 43,000 troops from 40 countries. In 2003 Afghanistan received an estimated US$191 million in foreign military assistance; in 2005 that figure was US$396 million. A 2008 U.S. proposal would expend a total of US$20 billion developing the Afghan armed forces and reorganizing occupation forces between 2009 and 2013. The Organization for Security and Co-operation in Europe (OSCE), of which Afghanistan became a cooperative partner in 2003, has an ongoing advisory program on security along the Tajikistan border.

External Threat: The major external threat is the movement of hostile forces, military matériel, and terrorists from staging areas across Afghanistan's porous borders. After occurring regularly since 2002, such movement from Pakistan accelerated in 2006 and 2007. Beginning in 2007, clandestine arms shipments across the Iran border also were identified.

Defense Budget: Between 2003 and 2007, the estimated military expenditure increased from US$61 million to US$161 million. The figure for 2006 was US$142 million.

Major Military Units: In 2007 Afghanistan's 35,000 military troops were stationed in regional commands in Gardez, Herat, Mazar-e Sharif, and Kandahar, and in a central command in Kabul. Plans called for each of those posts to have one corps. However, in 2007 only the corps in Kandahar and Kabul had a full complement of three brigades; the other commands consisted of only one or two brigades each.

Major Military Equipment: Amounts and distribution of equipment, mostly Soviet-manufactured, are not known. In 2007 the army had main battle tanks, reconnaissance vehicles, armored infantry fighting vehicles, armored personnel carriers, towed artillery, multiple rocket launchers, mortars, surface-to-surface missiles, recoilless rifles, antiaircraft guns, and surface-to-air missiles. The air force had six combat aircraft and seven support aircraft, to which it added in 2007 six Mi–17 transport helicopters, six Mi–35 helicopter gunships, and four An–32 transport aircraft.

Military Service: Males are eligible for conscription at age 22, and volunteers may enlist at age 18. The term of service for conscripts is four years.

Paramilitary Forces: Plans call for a border guard force of 12,000, which was not yet in existence in 2008.

Foreign Military Forces: Until September 2008, the coalition of foreign troops fighting Taliban and al Qaeda forces in Afghanistan was divided into two major commands: the U.S.-led Operation Enduring Freedom (OEF) and the North Atlantic Treaty Organization (NATO)–led International Security Assistance Force (ISAF). For the first time in 2008, the OEF command was united with that of the ISAF, to improve force coordination. Some missions of the two forces continued to diverge, however. In 2008 about 19,000 U.S. troops had remained in the OEF, while 15,100 were assigned to the ISAF. Between 2005 and 2008, the ISAF increased from 9,000 troops to about 43,000, a number to which 40 countries contributed. Besides the United States, in 2008 the major contributing countries, in order of contingent size, were Britain, Germany, Canada, Italy, the Netherlands, and France. Previously concentrated in northern and western Afghanistan, in 2006 ISAF forces began moving into the southern province of Helmand and the central province of Uruzgan. The 2006 Afghanistan Compact called for NATO troops to remain through 2010 or until the Afghan armed forces reach their planned troop levels. In 2006 President Karzai forecast that Afghanistan would need some foreign troops for 10 more years.

Police: Increasingly after 2002, the police were the only defense for civilians against insurgent forces in many parts of the country. Thus police duties often include paramilitary activities that are vital to national defense. Plans call for Afghanistan to increase its police force, the Afghan National Police (ANP), to 82,000, including conventional, border, highway, and counternarcotics police, by 2010. The force, which had an estimated 75,000 members in 2008, was to include members of all ethnic and tribal groups. Germany initiated the restoration program in 2002, and the European Union took over in 2007; in 2008 some 200 European trainers were in Afghanistan. However, the program has been handicapped by low pay, low recruit quality, pervasive corruption, and the insecure environment; in 2007 an estimated 925 police were killed, often by insurgents. According to a 2008 report, none of the 433 police units that have been trained is fully ready to face insurgent forces. In 2006 a U.S. interagency report stated that funding and assistance must continue beyond 2010 to establish a self-sustaining force. In 2008 a U.S. team initiated a district-level police program aimed at improving the quality of trainees. Although the police officially are responsible for maintaining civil order, local and regional military commanders continue to exercise control in the hinterland. The Afghan Customs Department, under the Ministry of Finance, operates 13 border customs stations in a system that is being modernized with international aid.

Internal Threat: In 2008 a large part of the country remained without adequate security, and armed bands launched attacks in regions not controlled by the central government. Reportedly, in 2007 the number of violent incidents increased by one-third over 2006, killing about 6,500 combatants and 1,500 civilians. In 2007 the number of suicide attacks increased from 123 to 160, and the number of roadside bombings increased from 1,931 to 2,615. Several extremist antigovernment groups maintained a substantial presence in Afghanistan in 2008. They included surviving members of the Taliban, al Qaeda operatives, and the Hezb-e Islami Gulbuddin, led by warlord Gulbuddin Hekmatyar, whom the United States designated a global terrorist in 2003. In 2004 the international medical organization Doctors without Borders withdrew its aid workers from Afghanistan when five members were killed, and in the years that followed other international nongovernmental organizations periodically suspended operations. In the first half of 2008, some 16 international aid workers were abducted and 12 killed.

A major internal security factor has been criminal and terrorist activity associated with the prosperous drug trade. Drug-processing laboratories are located throughout the country, traditional informal financial networks launder narcotics profits, and some provincial and national government officials have been implicated in the drug trade. After a small decrease in 2005, Afghanistan's opium output increased by 59 percent in 2006 and by 34 percent in 2007. Forcible eradication of poppy crops has caused controversy between Western policymakers and the Karzai government, and Western troops have been reluctant to antagonize local populations by eradication measures. Some government agencies have been implicated in the protection of the opium trade.

Terrorism: Between 2002 and 2008, President Karzai suffered four assassination attempts during which some government officials were killed. The latest such attack occurred in April 2008. Small-scale attacks on villages were common throughout the early 2000s. Large-scale terrorist attacks were rare in 2004 and 2005, but beginning in 2006 incidents increased in the south and southeast as larger Western forces entered southern territory dominated by insurgents and narcotics traffickers. Some 160 suicide bombings were reported in 2007, and several foreigners were kidnapped that year. In July 2008, a suicide bomber killed 41 people at the Indian Embassy in Kabul, the deadliest such attack since 2001.

Human Rights: The Bonn Agreement of 2001 established the Afghan Independent Human Rights Commission (AIHRC) to investigate human rights abuses and war crimes. In 2005 the government passed an ambitious, three-year Action Plan on Peace, Reconciliation and Justice in Afghanistan, whose goals were supposed to be met by the end of 2008. Those goals included documentation of crimes committed since the Soviet invasion of 1979, prosecution of human rights violators, and compensation of victims' families. However, as of mid-2008 the government had made only piecemeal progress toward fulfilling the plan. In the early 2000s, some types of human rights violations continued, particularly outside the region controlled by the central government. The National Security Directorate, Afghanistan's national security agency, has been accused of running its own prisons, torturing suspects, and harassing journalists. The security forces of local militias, which also have their own prisons, have been accused of torture and arbitrary killings. Warlords in the north have used property destruction, rape, and murder to discourage displaced Pashtuns from reclaiming their homes. Child labor and trafficking in people remain common outside Kabul. Civilians frequently have been killed in battles between warlord forces. A prison rehabilitation program began in 2003, but poor conditions in the overcrowded prisons have contributed to illness and death among prisoners. In the absence of an effective national judicial system, the right to judicial protection has been compromised as uneven local standards have prevailed in criminal trials.

The government has limited freedom of the media by selective crackdowns that invoke Islamic law, and self-censorship of the media has been encouraged. The media remain substantially government-owned. In 2004 a media law nominally lifted restrictions on some media activity but continued to forbid criticizing Islam or insulting officials. Journalists and legal experts criticized the nominally lesser restrictions of the 2004 law, and harassment and threats continued in 2008, especially outside Kabul. The commission that oversees the press includes no representatives of the news media, and the press law permits government censorship of the news. No registration of religious groups is required; minority religious groups are able to practice freely but not to proselytize.

Women's right to work outside the home, including political activity, has received increasing acceptance in the early 2000s. The constitution of 2004 makes an explicit commitment to the advancement of women and to gender equality, and 25 percent of the seats in the lower house of the National Assembly are designated for women. However, conservative elements in the judiciary have demanded separate education and a strict dress code for women. In rural areas, the social status of women remains low. They are denied access to education and jobs and often not allowed to leave their homes without a male relative. An estimated 80 percent of Afghan women enter forced marriages. In the early 2000s, poverty forced many women to enter the sex trade; their number is believed to have increased significantly since 2001, when it was estimated at 25,000.